My
Chocolate Bar
and other foods

W
FRANKLIN WATTS
LONDON·SYDNEY

First published in 2014 by
Franklin Watts
338 Euston Road
London
NW1 3BH

Franklin Watts Australia
Level 17/207 Kent Street
Sydney
NSW 2000

Copyright © Franklin Watts 2014

HB ISBN 978 1 4451 3276 1
Library ebook ISBN 978 1 4451 3278 5

A CIP catalogue record for this book is available from the British Library.

Series Editor: Julia Bird
Packaged by: Q2A Media

Picture credits:
Front Cover: Kesu, Nicram Sabod, Ammit Jack, AlephStudio, Stockyimages, Marco mayer/Shutterstock. Back Cover: Africa924/Shutterstock. Title page: Madlen, Kesu, Troyker, Joloei, Valentyn Volkov, Evgeny Karandaev, S-F, Sunsetman/Shutterstock. Imprint Page: Picsfive, Madlen, Sunsetman, Maks Narodenko, Horiyan/Shutterstock. P4(L): Marcus Lyonss/Fairtrade Ireland, P4(R):FairTrade International; P5: Ekler/Shutterstock; P6(R): Tristan Tan/Shutterstock, P6(L): Sursad/Shutterstock; P7(T): TongChuwit/Shutterstock; P7(B): Twin Design/Shutterstock; P8(T): FairTrade International; P8(C): Divine Chocolate Ltd; P8(B): Marie-Amelie Ormieres/Max Havelaar Belgium/Fairtrade International; P9(T): Divine Chocolate Ltd; P9(B): Kim Naylor/ Divine Chocolate Ltd; P10: Panom/Shutterstock; P11(T): Muriel Lasure/Shutterstock, P11(B): Paul J Martin/ Shutterstock; P12 Chris Pole/Shutterstock; P13(T): Eduardo Martino/Documentography/FairTrade International; P13(B):TongChuwit/Shutterstock; P14: Daniel J. Rao/Shutterstock; P15(T): F9photos/Shutterstock; P15(B): PavelSvoboda/Shutterstock; P16(B): Clipper teas.com; P16(T): TongChuwit/Shutterstock; P16(C): FairTrade International; P17(T): Jean Luc Lucien/T'Classic (Darjeeling) Pvt. Ltd; P17(B): Matt Gibson/Shutterstock; P18: RichardThornton/Shutterstock; P19: Xuanhuongho/Shutterstock; P20(TL): Cora Mueller/Shutterstock; P20(C): Jeremy Horner/Nomad/Corbis; P20(CR): FairTrade International; P20(BR): Chooseliberation.com; P21(T): TongChuwit/Shutterstock; P21(B): Simon de trey-White; P22:Samuel Borges Photography/Shutterstock; P22-23(Bgrnd): Happystock/Shutterstock; P23(T):Hywit Dimyadi/Shutterstock; P23(B): Elena Schweitzer/Shutterstock; P24(Bgrnd): Veron_ice/Shutterstock; P24(BL): The Turtle Factory/Shutterstock; P24 (TR): FairTrade International; P24(CR): Naturalbeverages; P25: Jose Manuel Gomez/Fairtrade International; P26: Alex Staroseltsev/ Shutterstock; P26-27(Bgrnd): Ramona Kaulitzki/Shutterstock; P27(B): Traidcraft; P27(T): Darios/shutterstock; P27 (C): FairTrade International; P28: Darios/shutterstock; P29(T): Felix Rohan/Shutterstock; P29(B): AndreyKlepikov/ Shutterstock; P30-31(Bgrnd): Tatyana Vyc/Shutterstock; P31: Picsfive, Madlen, Sunsetman, Maks Narodenko, Horiyan/Shutterstock; P32:Olha Afanasieva/Shutterstock. Illustrations: all-free-downloads.com (P4, 10, 12, 14-15, 26)

Printed in Malaysia

Franklin Watts is a division of Hachette Children's Books, an Hachette UK company. www.hachette.co.uk

Contents

Words in **bold** can be found in the glossary on page 30.

Why buy Fairtrade food?

How often do you look at the packaging around the foods that you eat?
Have you ever noticed the FAIRTRADE Mark?

What does the FAIRTRADE Mark mean?

The FAIRTRADE Mark was first added to food products, such as cocoa, tea and sugar, in 1994. The FAIRTRADE Mark shows that the product has been certified by the Fairtrade Foundation. This confirms that the food has been sourced from farmers who follow Fairtrade practices that are recognised around the world. This includes paying farmers a fair price for the work they do and the goods they produce.

FAIRTRADE

Guarantees a better deal for Third World Producers

FAIRTRADE

For a product to carry the FAIRTRADE Mark, all ingredients that can be, must be Fairtrade. That means the sugar in a chocolate bar, and ingredients, such as vanilla, dried fruit or nuts, will be Fairtrade too.

This is a FAIRTRADE Mark. It shows that the product is certified to offer a better deal to the farmers and workers involved in producing it.

What is the Fairtrade Foundation?

Big companies make huge profits selling us food, but the small farmers and workers who produce the food often struggle to make a living. The Fairtrade Foundation is a UK organisation that aims to get a fairer deal for farmers and workers in **developing countries**. When you buy Fairtrade foods, you know that farmers will receive a fair price for what they grow plus a little extra, the Fairtrade premium, which will go towards supporting projects that help the local community where the food is produced, and to protecting the environment where they live. In many countries, such as the US, Australia and Japan, there are different fair trade organisations.

This map shows the places mentioned in this book that are involved with Fairtrade food.

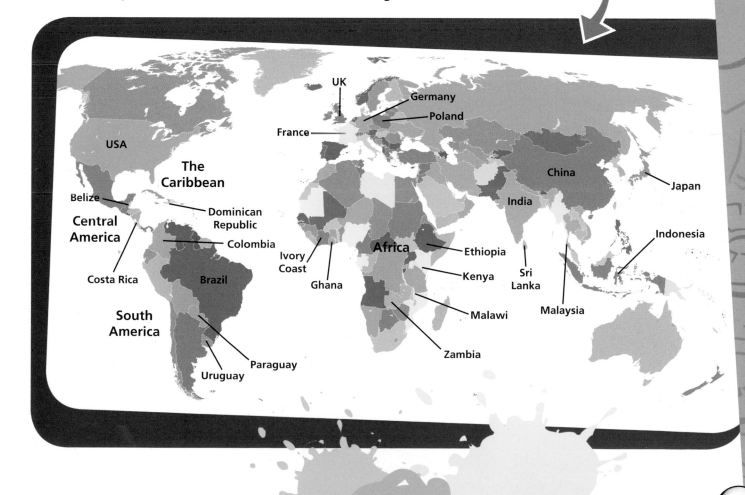

Chocolate

Almost £50 billion worth of chocolate is produced and sold each year. It is made from the cocoa bean.

Where does cocoa grow?

Cocoa comes from the cocoa bean, which grows inside a large pod, or fruit. Cocoa trees thrive in hot, wet, tropical rainforests. These trees first grew in South America and still grow there today, but now 70 per cent of the world's cocoa is grown in Africa. Between them, the West African countries of Ghana and the Ivory Coast produce over two million tonnes of cocoa a year.

seed pod

cocoa beans

Cocoa beans grow on trees in huge cocoa farms. Before they are made into chocolate, the beans taste very bitter.

How is cocoa turned into chocolate?

Workers harvest the cocoa pods by cutting them open with sharp knives and taking out the beans. On small farms the beans are left to **ferment** by wrapping them in banana leaves. On bigger farms they have different ways of fermenting the beans, such as leaving them in wooden boxes. The beans are then dried in the sun.

The dried beans are collected and shipped to the chocolate manufacturer. Here the beans are roasted and turned into a paste, butter or powder, which the manufacturer mixes with sugar, milk and other ingredients to make chocolate.

Re-use, recycle

For every tonne of cocoa, 10 tonnes of cocoa **husks** go to waste. A British paper manufacturer has come up with a way to use those husks – by turning them into chocolate wrappers!

Cocoa beans are made into liquid chocolate at a factory, before being turned into chocolate bars.

Special treatment

Many workers on cocoa plantations cannot afford health care if they become ill and may have to travel a long way to their nearest hospital. Some do not get the treatment they need in time and die. The Kavokiva **co-operative** was founded by 600 farmers in 1999, in the southeast of the Ivory Coast. Previously, up to 30 Kavokiva farmers died each year through injury or ill-health, so as well as paying a higher price for members' cocoa beans and providing financial support for fertilisers, pesticides and school fees, the co-operative also pays medical expenses.

One of Kavokiva's biggest achievements has been financing its own health centre with a doctor, midwife and two nurses so that patients don't have to travel a long way to a public hospital. Workers also have a free health insurance scheme with affordable medicines available to all members.

Good buy!

FAIRTRADE ®

Divine, the world's first Fairtrade chocolate company, was launched in 1998. Divine Chocolate Ltd give the farmers from Kuapa Kokoo in Ghana (see opposite), who grow the cocoa, a 45 per cent share in the company. They have a great motto: 'Pa Pa Paa', which means 'the best of the best'.

Customer demand is making Fairtrade chocolate more popular, and famous chocolates, such as Dairy Milk and Maltesers, now contain Fairtrade cocoa.

Divine Chocolate is sold in the UK and Australia and many other countries around the world.

At Kavokiva they have their own ambulance to collect patients from their villages. This has saved many lives.

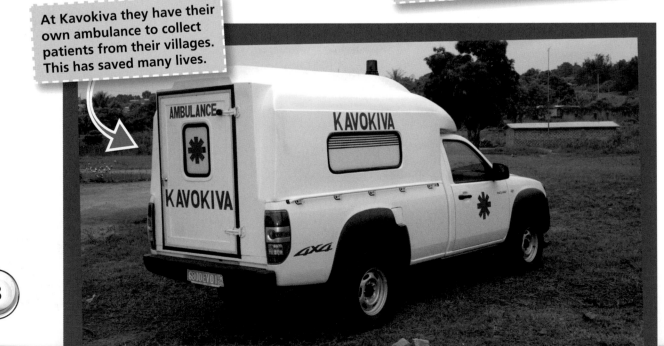

Case study: Kuapa Kokoo, Ghana

Jennifer's family belongs to the Kuapa Kokoo co-operative. Over 80,000 small-scale cocoa farmers work for this co-operative. The cocoa they sell can always be traced back where it was grown. The co-operative knows whether or not the producers have been following Fairtrade practices. If the co-operative finds children working unfairly, this will be checked and stopped.

School and summer camp

Thanks to the co-operative, Jennifer can go to school in her village and attend a summer camp to learn all about Fairtrade, the cocoa business, and the rights of workers. This year she was able to try some of the chocolate made from Kuapa Kokoo cocoa beans for the very first time.

This is Jennifer at the school the Kuapa Kokoo co-operative paid for.

Bananas

Bananas are some of the most famous Fairtrade products. Around one in three bananas sold in the UK is a Fairtrade banana.

Banana plants grow on stems which are 3 to 8 metres tall. The clusters of fruits grow upside down in bunches, known as 'hands'. Each hand contains around 10 bananas and there are 3 to 6 hands in a bunch.

Where do bananas grow?

Bananas grow in over 150 countries around the world. These countries are hot, with plenty of rainfall, because banana plants need a lot of moisture from the soil. You might have eaten bananas grown in Costa Rica, the Dominican Republic or the eastern Caribbean. In most countries the plantations are small and owned and managed by a family rather than a big corporation.

How do bananas grow?

Bananas grow quickly and can be **harvested** all year round. A **sucker** is planted in the ground and eight to twelve months later the bananas can be harvested. One slice of a **machete** chops off a heavy stem of green bananas. The bananas are washed, checked for quality, stickered and packed into boxes.

In some plantations, workers carry whole stems of bananas on their heads or shoulders. In others, a system of pulleys saves workers' aching backs.

How do bananas get to our shops?

Green bananas have to be handled very carefully – if they bruise, they won't sell. They are transported in refrigerated ships, called reefers, and kept at a temperature of 13.3°C. It can take many days for the ship to reach the country where the bananas are going to be sold.

Refrigerated ships like this carry bananas and other fruit around the world. The bananas are kept cool to stop them from ripening. On arrival at their destination, the bananas are ripened in specialist warehouses.

Chemical hazard

Today, banana producers can grow two or three times as many bananas as they did in the 1960s. They do this partly with the help of **agrochemicals** that help to kill pests and diseases. But some of these chemicals are **toxic**, and can affect the health of the plantation workers. Fairtrade bananas are **regulated**, to ensure the workers are not at risk from these chemicals. Because of this, Fairtrade encourages **organic** farmers who use natural **fertilisers**.

Plastic covers

Farmers often cover their bananas with plastic bags to protect them from insects, diseases and strong wind. In the past, the plastic was carelessly thrown away and some of the bags, which had been treated with chemicals, could end up in the rivers and pollute the water. This was bad for the environment. Now, farmers who join Fairtrade recycle the plastic bags because of the damage they they can do to the environment.

Environment matters

In Costa Rica, **pesticides** from non-organic banana crops could be causing trouble. Heavy rains wash the pesticides into nearby rivers, causing pollution. As a result, local caiman populations could be under threat. A report claimed that caimans, a type of crocodile, living near non-organic banana plantations, were 50 per cent thinner than this healthy one.

Case study: Coobafrio co-op, Colombia, South America

In the 1990s, Albeiro Alfonso Cantillo, or Foncho, as his friends call him, got together with 19 other farmers, to form a co-operative called Coobafrio. At the time, their businesses were hardly bringing in enough money to feed their families. Members hoped that by selling their bananas as a group, they could ask for a better price. The co-operative proved a success, and today it has 43 farmers who employ nearly 300 workers.

Coobafrio joined Fairtrade in 2011 and now two-thirds of their bananas are sold as Fairtrade. This means that $1.00 from each box is invested back into the business and the local community.

Protecting the environment

Following Fairtrade production methods, the co-op must make sure that local water sources are protected and waste is properly recycled. Coobafrio no longer uses chemicals on its bananas, instead it provides well-paid jobs for local people, who help out with weeding.

Fairtrade has helped 82 per cent of Coobafrio members to pay for school fees and uniforms for their children. Foncho thinks education is the very best way to keep his family out of poverty.

Foncho works very hard for the co-operative and for his family. He takes his daughter to university at 5am, then returns to work on his banana farm till 6pm.

Re-use, recycle

Before **composting** your banana skin, use it to polish your shoes! Rub the inside of the skin all over your leather shoe, then polish it off with a clean cloth. The natural oils in the banana skin help to make leather shine.

Tea

On average, people around the world drink 70,000 cups of tea every second!

Where does tea come from?

According to an old story, over 4,800 years ago, a tea leaf dropped into the Chinese Emperor Shennong's bowl of hot water and made the first cup of tea. Today, China is still the world's biggest producer of tea, closely followed by India, Sri Lanka and Kenya.

How is tea produced?

The leaves of the tea shrub are picked by hand all year round by field workers. The bags are weighed and taken to a **processing plant** nearby, where the leaves are withered, rolled and then fermented. The leaves need to be processed quickly, to make sure the quality stays high.

Workers line up to have the tea they have picked weighed. Some tea workers who are not part of Fairtrade earn less than 75 pence a day. The World Bank calls this living on the poverty line.

Hard workers

Most of the workers on tea plantations are children and women. They are expected to carry heavy baskets or bags on their backs, often in scorching heat. On non-Fairtrade plantations women are usually paid less than men even though they may work longer hours. The women are often bullied and threatened by their bosses and the children may not receive any education.

Only the uppermost leaves and shoots are picked from the tea bushes. Fairtrade tea is grown without using harmful chemical fertilisers and

Women picking tea carry heavy baskets that hold the tea leaves. They may have to stand for hours in the hot sun.

Fairtrade is working with tea plantation owners in India and Africa to make sure the workers are treated with respect and paid a fair wage. The **Fairtrade premium** that they receive is helping to pay for new roads, to make sure that local villages have clean water and that there are health clinics within the plantations.

Re-use, recycle

Used teabags can help a bruise to heal faster, or soothe your eyes when they're feeling tired. Remember to let the teabags cool first!

Good buy!

The Clipper Tea Company was founded in 1984, when an English couple started to sell tea from Assam in India to local shops. Twenty years later, the Clipper Tea Company was producing two million organic tea bags a day, in 95 varieties. Clipper's teabags are all Fairtrade. When Clipper tea buyers find a tea estate they like, the first questions they ask are about how the workers are treated.

What about coffee?

When the price of coffee dropped in 1997, many small farmers suffered. Some began earning less than 1p per cup despite the huge profits earned by the big name coffee chains – some farmers even began losing money. Fairtrade coffee earns coffee farmers a much better income, which they can use to benefit their workers, their community and the local environment. In 2009, the Starbucks coffee chain became the largest buyer of Fairtrade coffee in the world.

Case study: Makaibari Tea Estate, Darjeeling, India

In Makaibari, a Fairtrade estate, life has been a little easier since each family on the tea estate was given their own cow. The family drinks the cow's milk, and manure from the cow is turned into **renewable bio-gas** for cooking. There is also extra money to be made by selling leftover milk and manure.

Women workers in control

The Makaibari Estate has 25 women supervisors, which is unusual. An elected group of women decides how community funds should be spent. The estate provides education for its workers, as well as protection for the local environment.

Makaibari now has a computer centre that helps to educate over 78 children. It also funds **scholarships** to send local children to study **horticulture**.

Seventy per cent of the Makaibari Estate has been left as forest so **endangered** animals, such as this leopard, are able to thrive there.

Peanuts

Peanuts are among the world's most popular nuts. People in the USA alone eat around 270 million kilograms of peanuts each year.

Peanuts are one of the most important crops grown in the developing world.

Where do peanuts come from?

Fossils of peanut shells, found in South America, show that people were growing and eating peanuts over 7,000 years ago. Explorers and traders took the peanut plant to Africa in the 16th century, and by the beginning of the 17th century peanuts were growing in China, Japan, Malaysia and Indonesia. Although they still grow in all these countries, the main producers are now China, India and the USA. In Africa, peanuts are known as 'groundnuts', because they grow underground.

Hard workers

Most of the workers on tea plantations are children and women. They are expected to carry heavy baskets or bags on their backs, often in scorching heat. On non-Fairtrade plantations women are usually paid less than men even though they may work longer hours. The women are often bullied and threatened by their bosses and the children may not receive any education.

Women picking tea carry heavy baskets that hold the tea leaves. They may have to stand for hours in the hot sun.

Only the uppermost leaves and shoots are picked from the tea bushes. Fairtrade tea is grown without using harmful chemical fertilisers and

Fair price for tea

Fairtrade is working with tea plantation owners in India and Africa to make sure the workers are treated with respect and paid a fair wage. The **Fairtrade premium** that they receive is helping to pay for new roads, to make sure that local villages have clean water and that there are health clinics within the plantations.

Re-use, recycle

Used teabags can help a bruise to heal faster, or soothe your eyes when they're feeling tired. Remember to let the teabags cool first!

Good buy!

The Clipper Tea Company was founded in 1984, when an English couple started to sell tea from Assam in India to local shops. Twenty years later, the Clipper Tea Company was producing two million organic tea bags a day, in 95 varieties. Clipper's teabags are all Fairtrade. When Clipper tea buyers find a tea estate they like, the first questions they ask are about how the workers are treated.

What about coffee?

When the price of coffee dropped in 1997, many small farmers suffered. Some began earning less than 1p per cup despite the huge profits earned by the big name coffee chains – some farmers even began losing money. Fairtrade coffee earns coffee farmers a much better income, which they can use to benefit their workers, their community and the local environment. In 2009, the Starbucks coffee chain became the largest buyer of Fairtrade coffee in the world.

How are peanuts grown and harvested?

The peanut plant grows to about 45 cm tall. Its flowers appear above the soil, while the nuts grow underneath. Peanuts are ready for harvesting four or five months after planting. Workers dig the plants out of the ground.

The peanuts are stripped from the plant by hand, one pod at a time.

Case study: Co-operative Pueblo Apicola, Uruguay

In 2006, thirty small, family-run honey farms in Uruguay started working together as the Pueblo Apicola co-operative. In 2010, the co-operative was certified one of only 12 Fairtrade honey producers in the world. Before the co-operative existed, the farmers had to sell their honey to a representative, who paid them far less than their honey was worth.

Apicola actually means 'honey producer' and the honey the co-operative produces is collected from 6,000 hives placed in 180,000 hectares of eucalyptus forest. The eucalyptus gives the honey a delicious, lemony flavour.

Loans and training

Exported honey has to meet Fairtrade standards, and the production, storage and transportation processes are strictly monitored. However, Fairtrade has helped the farmers with loans to support their businesses, and gives special training, for example, in producing organic honey.

Buyers pay a Fairtrade Premium for Apicola's honey and so far this has been used to provide training for workers on the co-operative. The money also pays for farmers to attend trade fairs, where they can find new markets for their produce.

Bee keepers inspect their hives regularly to make sure the bees are healthy. In high summer there can be as many as 35,000 bees in a beehive, which drops to around 5,000 in winter.

Pesticides killing bees

One third of all the food we produce relies on **pollination** by bees and other insects. One estimate claims that the work bees do each year, pollinating crops around the world, is worth 265 billion euros! But around the world bees are dying out. Losing bees could seriously affect the production of 75 per cent of the crops we rely on, including apples, strawberries and tomatoes.

No one knows for certain what is causing the bees to die, but pesticides, climate change and farming systems that produce only one crop could all be contributing to the problem.

Pesticide ban

In 2013, the European Union (EU) placed a two-year ban on certain pesticides that are thought to be harming the bee population. Greenpeace is also asking the EU to support ecological farming practices, including organic farming, as well as improving conservation and increasing research into farming methods that will encourage and protect bees.

Even wild bees can be exposed to pesticides and, as natural habitats are increasingly lost, experts worry that we may start losing many of the plants that rely on bee pollination, too.

Glossary

agrochemicals Chemicals used in agriculture to prevent diseases and kill insects. They can be dangerous to humans

bio-gas Gas produced from decaying matter, such as manure or rubbish

borehole A hole drilled into the earth. Sometimes these are made to find safe drinking water, or to extract gas or oil

composting Letting organic waste material, such as banana skins, rot to make compost that is then used to improve the quality of the soil to help things grow better

co-operative A group of people, or organisations, working together and sharing any benefits or profits evenly between them

developing countries Parts of the world that are not well off, but are using their resources to build up different industries

endangered When an animal or species is at serious risk of dying out or becoming extinct

Fairtrade Premium An additional sum of money paid for Fairtrade goods that is used to benefit the local community

ferment A chemical change in something, for example in tea leaves as they dry

fertiliser A natural or chemical substance that is spread over soil to help plants grow

fossils The remains in rock of animals or plants that lived on Earth millions of years ago

harvested When crops are gathered at the end of the growing season

horticulture The growing of fruits, vegetables or plants

husks The dry outer covering of a seed, such as the cocoa pod

machete A knife with a long, wide, sharp blade used in agriculture

nectar A sweet liquid that bees collect from flowers

organic Food that is produced without using chemical fertilisers

pesticide A chemical used to kill insects or small animals

pollination When bees carry pollen from one flower to another so that new plants can grow

processing

Websites

Visit the FAIRTRADE website to find out more about Fairtrade, and the products you can buy:
www.fairtrade.net
www.fairtrade.org.uk

What's so special about the Dubble chocolate bar? Find out here:
www.dubble.co.uk
Here's more about Divine chocolate:
www.divinechocolate.com

Find out about ASOBANU bananas here:
www.fairtrade.org.uk/resources/films/bananas_dominican_republic.aspx
There's even more information about bananas here:
www.bananalink.org.uk

Discover the full story of Clipper teas here:
www.clipper-teas.com/our-story/who-we-are
Find out how Liberation Foods started, and meet some of the farmers who have benefitted from working with them:
www.chooseliberation.com

Find out about Ubuntu Cola here:
www.ubuntu-trading.com/our-fairtrade-cola
In New Zealand, Karma Cola is another fair trade fizzy drink. Find out about how it started and who it's helping:
www.allgoodorganics.co.nz/karma-cola/

There's lots more about sugar here:
www.sucrose.com/lcane.html

Lots more information on Fairtrade honey here:
www.fairtrade.net/honey.html

Every effort has been made by the Publishers to ensure that the websites are suitable for children, and that they contain no inappropriate or offensive material. However, because of the nature of the Internet, it is impossible to guarantee that the contents of these sites will not be altered. We strongly advise that Internet access is supervised by a responsible adult.

Index